PERFECTLY IMPERFECT

SONA L. NOBLE

Perfectly Imperfect
by Sona L. Noble
Published by One Faith Publishing
Richmond, VA, Port Huron, MI
onefaithpublishings@gmail.com

Table of Contents

Dedication

This book is dedicated to my children, Ebony, Jaycen, and Joy.

FOREWORD

We met at a moment when Sona was earnestly seeking answers, clarity, purpose, and the means to change the trajectory of her life. What began as a search for direction has grown into something far deeper: a powerful testimony of faith, resilience, and transformation.

Sona's story reaches back to tragic, yet humble beginnings. But she did not remain there.

Over time, she has become a devoted, teachable woman of our Heavenly Father, someone who has learned to trust the process, even when the road was painful or unclear.

Now, as Sona breaks her silence in this book, "Perfectly Imperfect," she shares the real-life account of her journey, its rising moments, its difficult seasons, and the unexpected "curveballs" life sometimes throws.

Her experiences will not only resonate with you but also guide you through your own trials and challenges. Reminding you that you truly can win when your faith is anchored in God. Because it isn't only about how life starts; it's about how the hand of the Father can steer, sustain, and navigate you through every chapter according to the path He has already set for you. And on that journey, happiness and satisfaction are possible even when things aren't perfect.

As a mentor and a friend, Sona Noble stands as living proof of what it means to be favored by the Lord, an Overcomer, and a Victorious testimony.

– Veronica Carouthers,

Atmosphere of Fire Ministries

My mentor: Veronica Carouthers

ACKNOWLEDGEMENT

Lily Jackson (Grandma)

You never gave up on me. Continue to rest in peace, my beautiful flower.

Pastor Shirley Hood (Mother in the Faith)

From the very first time I met you, you showed me genuine love. Your nurturing spirit is a blessing. You are truly a woman of Zion.

Prophetess Veronica Carouthers (Mentor)

The teachings and training you've poured into me are a true blessing. I'm always honored to be in your presence.

Elder Kevin Payton

Your encouragement and support mean more than words can express. You are truly a man of honor.

One Faith Publishing (Tammy Jae')

Your dedication and hard work have not gone unnoticed. Thank you for bringing my story to life.

Trauma

According to Merriman Webster, trauma is defined primarily as a serious bodily injury, such as a wound caused by external agent or an abnormal psychological behavioral state, resulting from severe emotional stress.

It also refers to the agent, force, or mechanism that causes such distress.

Chapter One

THE MURDER SCENE

"Do not fear [anything], for I am with you; Do not be afraid, for I am your God. I will strengthen you, be assured I will help you;

I will certainly take hold of you with My righteous right hand [a hand of justice, of power, of victory, of salvation].'
- Isaiah 41:10 (Amplified Bible)

I can vividly remember February 25, 1977, as if it were yesterday. What began as a normal weekend turned into something I would never forget. I was only 10 years old, a little girl who loved the color pink and playing with my favorite Barbie doll and her pink sports car.

It was an ordinary Saturday. My younger siblings, Subrina (7), Lady (4), and I were sitting together watching TV, and Durad (5), my brother, was spending the weekend with his father. I don't exactly remember what caused the argument between my Mama and Lester, but I do remember the fear I felt when he tried to hit her.

Without a second thought, something inside me shifted. I knew I had to protect her. So, I ran into the kitchen and grabbed a knife. As Lester sat in the dining room, I stabbed him in the thigh three or four times, and after the commotion was over, he left. This incident caused my Mama to have a neighbor come over quickly to change the locks on both the front and side doors.

The next day, February 26, something felt different from the start. It was cold, and there was an uneasiness in the air that even I, as a child, could feel. My mama was lying on the sofa, while my sisters and I sat on the loveseat by the window watching TV, and that's when I heard the sound of Lester's car pulling up.

He walked to the front door and realized the locks had been changed. Then he went to the side door and found that the lock had been changed as well. Angrily, he began yelling, "Lula, open the door!" My sisters and I sat there in fear. But my Mama tried to calm us down by saying, "Don't worry. Just be quiet, and he'll go away."

He did leave, but not for long.

Later, he returned with his son from a previous marriage, who appeared to be about the same age as my mama, who was 24 years old. The two of them got out of the car and began kicking the side door until it broke open. Once inside, I could hear their footsteps moving throughout the house, from the kitchen to the dining room, and then into the living room. As Lester approached the living room, I could see that he was holding a rifle.

My Mama quickly jumped up from the sofa, and after a brief exchange of words, she turned and ran up the stairs as he raised the rifle. Then the shots were fired, and he kept shooting until my mama fell down near the front door.

In that moment, I was sure I would be shot next.

But instead, Lester and his son turned and left out through the side door. After I heard the car drive away, I knew I had to help my Mama. So, I told my sisters I was going to get help. I looked out the window; it felt safe, so I quickly put on my shoes and coat and ran down the street to a neighbor's house.

When I got there, Miss Carroll asked me what was wrong. Through my tears and fear, I said, "My baby sister's father just shot my mama. I need help!" She immediately called 911. We didn't have a phone at home, and I didn't know anyone's number. But I later learned that Lester had already called my family and told them, "Y'all better go get the kids, because I just shot Lula."

Shortly after, the police arrived at Miss Carroll's house, and they took me back home. I couldn't stop crying. Over and over, I asked the officer if my mama was dead. The lady officer didn't answer me right away. Instead, she handed me a paper bag and told me to breathe in it because I was in shock.

Finally, the officers told me the truth. My mama was deceased. By then, my grandmother had arrived, and I remember overhearing an officer say the words, "This is a murder scene." Then the officers turned to me and said, "We need you to tell us exactly what happened."

My Siblings

Lady

Me (Sona)

Subrina

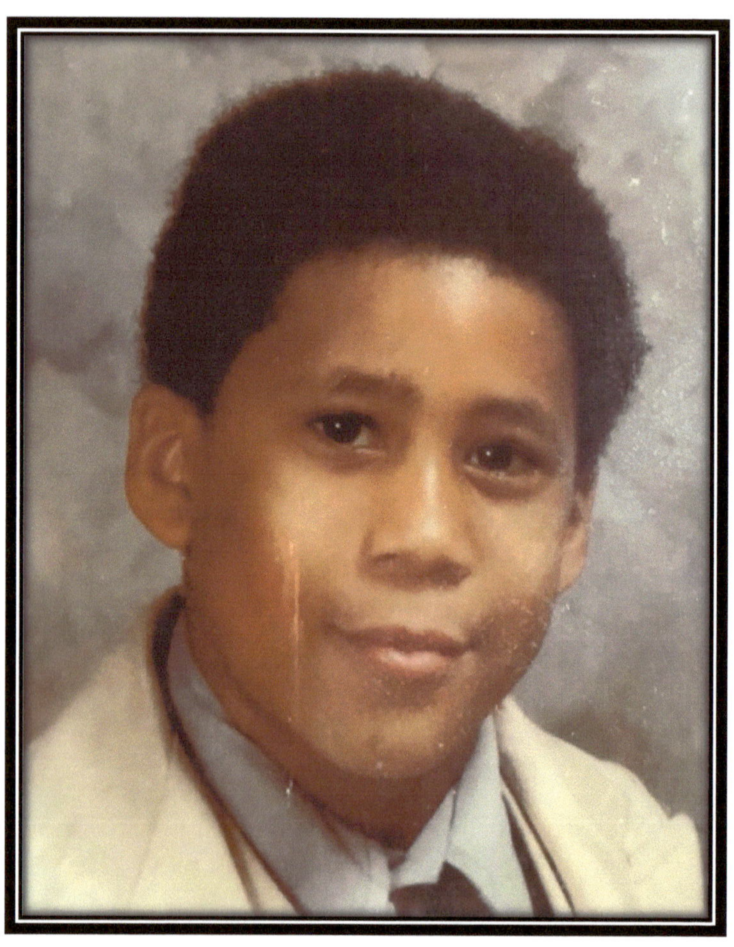

Durad

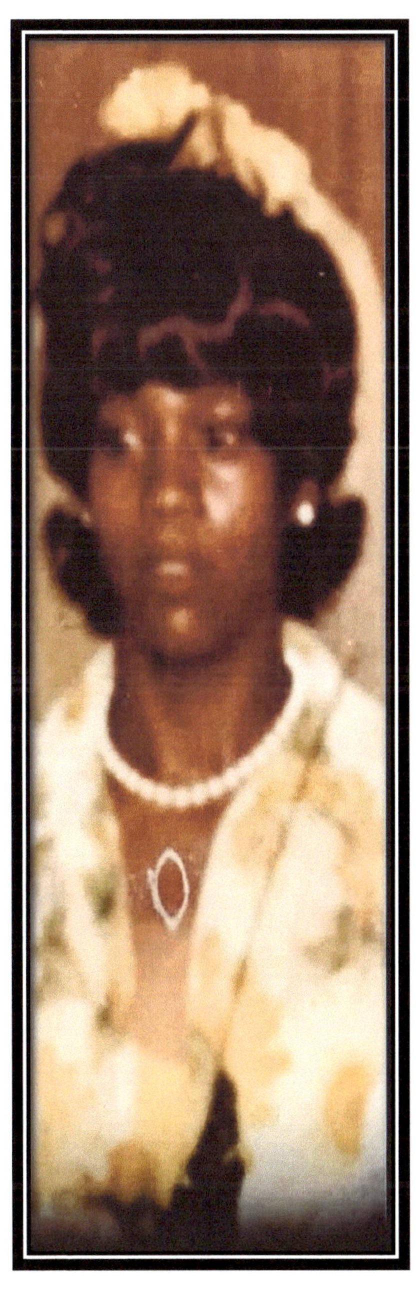

My Mama

Chapter 2

IN THE BEGINNING

"In him we were also chosen, having been predestined according to the plan of him who works out everything in conformity with the purpose of his will." - Ephesians 1:11 (NIV)

llow me to take you back to the beginning and where it all began… My grandparents, Roosevelt Noble and Lily Noble, were already divorced before I was born. During their marriage, the couple had four children: Larry, Lula, Joyce, and Lillie.

Life moved on, and my Grandma had two more children, Eloise and Robert Earl, before she met and married a man named Curtis Jackson.

Curtis Jackson was not only a man who would become my grandfather… but in a complicated way, he is also my great-uncle.

The story behind that connection is not simple.

As the story goes… Curtis Jackson, my grandmother, and her children lived in Port Huron, Michigan. One day, his nephew, Robert James Scruggs, from St. Louis, Missouri, came to visit.

As time passed, something happened that should never have happened. Robert James was in his twenties, and my mama was only thirteen years old when I was conceived. Because of my mama's age, Robert James was later sent to prison for statutory rape. That is how Curtis Jackson not only became my grandfather but also my great-uncle.

My family often told me I was a beautiful and very active baby. My aunts and uncles were still children themselves, ranging in age from nine to fifteen. Like most kids, they loved to play, and sometimes their idea of fun wasn't always the safest.

My aunts and uncles would toss me from one set of arms to another, laughing as they did. One would jokingly say, "I don't got her!" while passing me off to another, just like the game "Hot Potato." My Grandmother and Mama would laugh along, but always with a warning: "Y'all better not hurt her." I was too young to understand the danger I was in, but thankfully, I was never hurt.

Eventually, my grandparents separated, and not long after, my family moved to 192 Midland Street in Highland

Park, Michigan. Back then, Highland Park was known as the "City of Trees." It was a small place, less than three miles long, and it sat right in the middle of Detroit. That house on Midland Street holds some of my earliest and most memorable moments.

One of my first memories goes back to 1969, when my Mama walked through the front door holding my newborn baby sister, fresh home from the hospital. There was something about that moment that stayed with me, a feeling of warmth, of family, and of togetherness.

Another precious moment that has never left my memory is my nickname. I can't remember how I got the nickname, Tina Turner. But even though I knew my real name was Sonia, no one ever called me that because, to my family, I was their Tina Turner.

My family brought joy into my life because they knew exactly how to help bring that name to life. They would play the song *"Proud Mary"* and say, "Get it, Tina Turner!" And just like that, I would start shimmering just like Tina Turner. With this memory, I was about four years old.

Family time meant everything to my Grandmother, and she made sure we spent time together whenever we could. One day, we all went to an amusement park, and I remember being completely captivated by the cotton candy.

Without realizing it, I had wandered off without anyone noticing. But it didn't take long before someone noticed that I was gone, and the search began to find me. Eventually, my Uncle Larry found me unharmed and standing with a security guard. But when he saw the guard, something stopped him in his tracks… the security guard reminded him of his father, who had passed away three years earlier. And as we walked away, the security guard looked at my uncle and said, "Take care of my baby."

I was a very young child during that time, yet those memories remain so vivid. I may not understand how I can remember them so clearly, but I hold them close to my heart.

Because now I know…

God gave me laughter before the tears.

He gave me love before the loss.

He gave me memories that would one day remind me that my story did not begin in pain; it began in purpose.

So, when I think back to that house on 192 Midland Street, I don't just remember a place; I remember a loving home.

It was where my story began.

It was where love lived.

And for a time… it was where our world felt safe.

Curtis Jackson

(My grandfather and great-uncle)

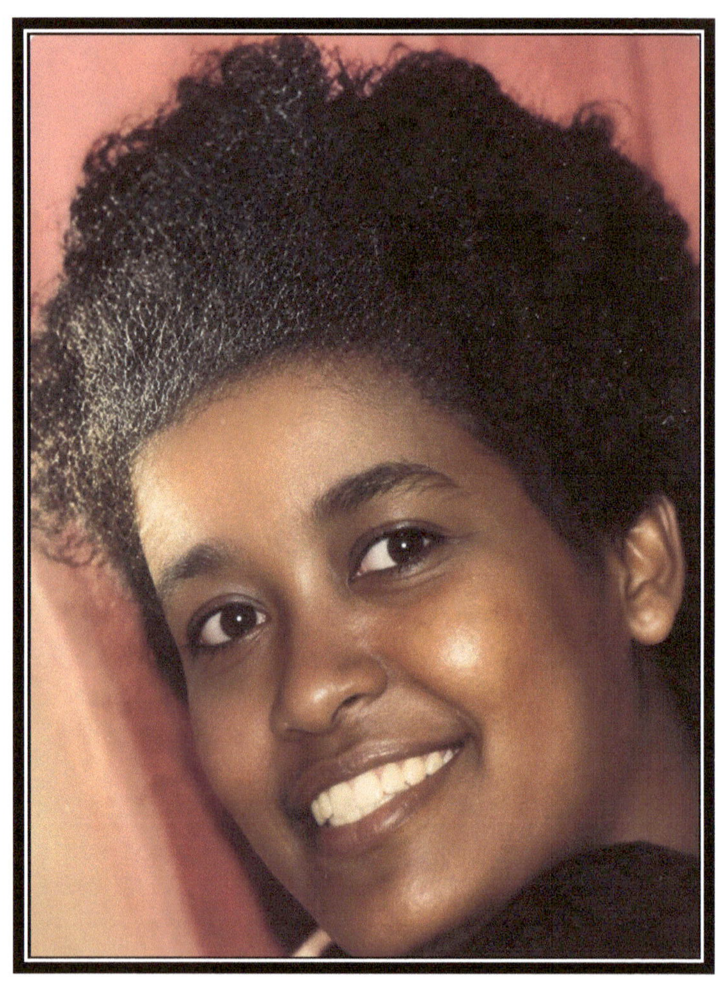

Lily Noble

(My grandmother)

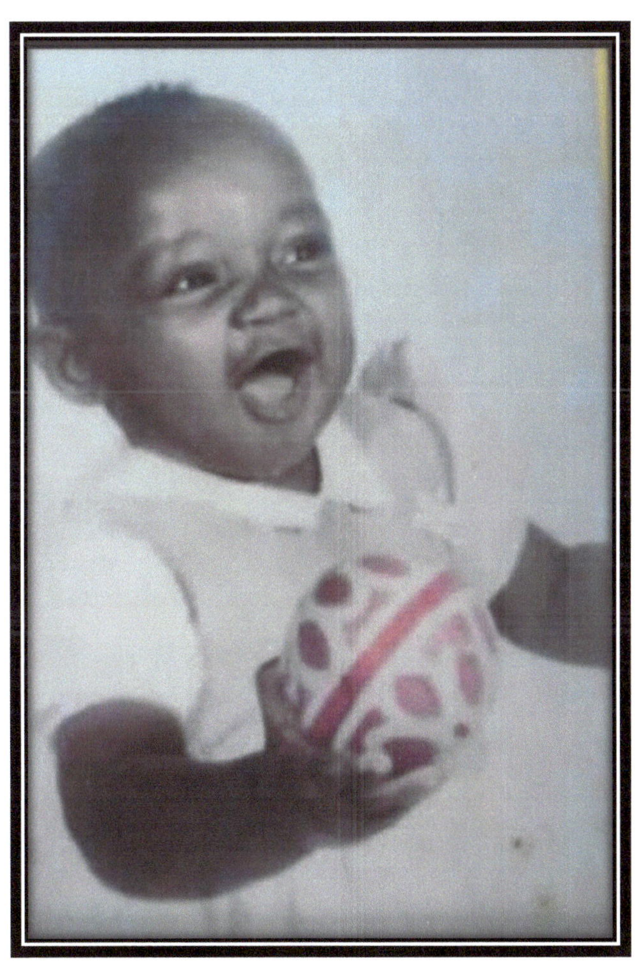

My Mama

Heavy King

ROOSEVELT NOBLE, who learned something about the manly art of self-defense as a Blue Water District Golden Glover some years back, has been crowned heavyweight champion of the Eilson AFB, Alaska.

A2/C Noble of 5039 Air Police Sqd., is the husband of Lillie B. Noble and son of Mrs. Helen Noble, 2728 —24th street.

Roosevelt Noble (My grandfather)

Chapter 3

I Was Silent

"For we wrestle not against flesh and blood, but against principalities, against powers, against the rulers of the darkness of this world, against spiritual wickedness in high places."
– Ephesians 6:12 (KJV)

My mama met Lester in 1971, when my little brother was still a toddler. Lester was short and dark-skinned with a short afro combed to the front. He seemed to be about twenty years older than my Mama. At the time, my Mama was only nineteen, average in height, slim, and she had a beautiful caramel complexion.

I remember Lester picking us up in his gold 1970 Cadillac Coupe de Ville, and what stood out the most was when he would call my Mama "Lola," even though her real name was Lula. For some reason, hearing him call her that name always seemed to irritate me. Around that same time, my mama was pregnant with my baby sister, Lady, and because she was pregnant, Lester began treating her like she was his prized possession.

Lester eventually rented a corner house on Alden Street. It was a small two-bedroom house; therefore, Subrina, Durad, and I all had to share one room. Durad slept in his crib, while Subrina and I slept in twin beds. When my baby sister was born in July of 1972, she slept in a bassinet in the room with my Mama and Lester.

On Christmas Day, I received a big dollhouse, an Easy-Bake Oven, and a Baby Alive doll. I was so excited that I began to think that maybe Lester wasn't so bad after all.

But that feeling didn't last for long.

Uncle Robert came over and installed a 100-watt light bulb in my Easy-Bake Oven, and together we made my very first cake.

Shortly after Christmas, Lester started coming in at night to tuck my sister and me into bed. But with every "tuck," I felt his hands touching me in ways that didn't feel right. I was confused and afraid at the same time. Deep down, I knew something was wrong, but I was too scared to say anything. So, it continued, and with every tuck, there was an inappropriate touch.

When spring arrived, all the kids in the neighborhood that was my age were riding bikes with training wheels, just like me. Then one day, I noticed that everyone had theirs taken off and was speeding right past me. I went home and told my Mama that I wanted my training wheels off, too. She looked at me, smiled, and said, “Okay.”

When Uncle Robert came over, he took the training wheels off my bike. I was filled with excitement to ride my bike on my own. My uncle told me he would hold on to the back of my seat as I started to pedal. But the moment he let go, I fell.

I began to whine, but my Mama said, "You okay?" And my uncle encouraged me by saying, “Get back up.”

On that day, I remember being so determined to get back up and learn how to ride my bike. So, I got back on it and tried again, and this time, I kept going. I was so excited that I didn’t need training wheels anymore.

As I look back, I can clearly understand that it wasn’t just about learning how to ride a bike. It was about learning how to move forward even after falling and how to trust myself.

Sometimes, God allows the “training wheels” in our lives to come off, not to harm us, but to show us that we are stronger, braver, and more capable than we ever imagined.

And even when we fall… we can get back up and keep going.

One day, while Lester was in our room "tucking us in," my Mama walked in and asked what he was doing. He replied, "I'm just tucking them in." I truly believe my mama had her suspicions, but she couldn't prove anything.

Another time, I don't remember what I had done, but I do remember Lester whooping me. He made sure the belt buckle hit my lip, leaving it swollen and bloody. The look in his eyes told me everything… *You better not tell.*

When my Mama got home, she put ice on my lip and asked Lester what happened. He said it was an accident. My Mama was upset and told him that he was never to whoop my sister or me again.

Not long after that, my Mama began asking me questions whenever Lester wasn't around. Over and over, she would ask if he had been touching my privates. But every time she asked, I told her no. Even though I kept Lester's secret, my Mama's instincts told her otherwise. She started keeping me close whenever Lester was home, and if she went to take a shower, I was right there with her.

One day, my mama had to go and handle some business, and she told me, "If I'm not home when you get out of school, go to the neighbor's house." I said, "Okay," but I didn't go there. Instead, when I got out of school and saw the door was locked, I made a different decision.

At just six years old, I had always paid attention, so I walked over a mile long to my Grandmother's house because I knew the way…down Puritan Street, then to Hamilton, and just two blocks over was my Grandma's street.

When I arrived, my Grandmother asked, "How did you get here?"

I looked at her and said, "I walked by myself."

She replied, "Baby, that's dangerous; you shouldn't have walked by yourself."

Shortly after, my Mama called, and my Grandmother told her I was there. When my Mama came to pick me up, she said, "Tina, I told you to go to the neighbor's house."

I didn't say a word. But in my mind, I knew one thing for certain… Grandma's house was the safest place to be.

A couple of years later, my Mama left Lester, and we moved to Port Huron. We lived in the new projects, and I was so glad to be away from him. Unfortunately, Lester would still drive from Detroit to Port Huron. It was a 45-

minute drive, but Lester would still come and visit, and all the while, he was really just trying to get my Mama back. And for the longest time, she didn't go back.

Then one day out of nowhere, my Mama asked me a question: "How would you feel if we moved back with Lester?"

I told her, "No, Mama. I just want it to be us!"

She asked me why, but I couldn't tell her the truth. I just said, "I don't like him."

Sadly, we moved back to Detroit with Lester. He got us a house on Cloverlawn Street, not far from Puritan. This time, it was a two-story house; my Mama's and Lester's bedrooms were downstairs, and Subrina, Lady, Durad, and I shared a room upstairs. But nothing stopped Lester from finding any excuse to come upstairs, and the touching started again.

By this time, I was ten years old, and one day after school, my Mama wasn't home, and I walked six miles to my grandmother's house. Even then… I knew what safe felt like, and it didn't matter how many miles it took to get there.

Uncle Robert

Chapter 4

LILY OF THE VALLEY

"The name of the LORD is a strong tower; The righteous run to it and are safe." – Proverbs 18:10 (New King James Version)

After I was questioned by the police, I looked at my Grandma and asked, "Can we go to your house?" She looked back at me and said, "Yes. Y'all are coming with me." And in that moment, she promised me that she would keep us together. Soon after, my Grandma began gathering a few of our belongings. I remember grabbing Mama's short and curly wig and her long green coat with the fur around the collar.

When we arrived at Grandma's house, I saw Auntie Eloise. I held up the coat and said, "This belongs to my Mama." With compassion in her eyes, she gently said, "We can hang her coat in the hall closet." Then I asked, "Where can I put her wig?"

Auntie Eloise handed me an orange sewing box, and I placed the wig inside. That small act made me feel like I was still protecting a piece of my Mama.

Unexpectedly, Subrina, Lady, and I were given the same bedroom that once belonged to Mama, so I put Mama's wig in our closet, and from time to time, I would smell her wig and pray, "God, please bring my mama back to life."

My Uncle Larry and Durad slept in the same room, and Auntie Eloise and her baby slept in another room. My Uncle Robert's room was in the attic, and he had to walk through our bedroom to get upstairs. There always seemed to be some sort of music coming down from his room: Norman Connors, Earth, Wind & Fire, and Kool & the Gang are the artists I can remember.

During that time, my Auntie Joyce and Auntie Lillie had already moved out and had homes and families of their own. Yet, Grandma's room was where we all gathered together. For some unknown reason, her room felt like the safest place in the entire house.

It wasn't long after moving in with my Grandma that I found myself becoming overly protective of my siblings. I began questioning anything and everything any adult said or did to them. And as a repercussion, I often heard, "They're not your children!" But what they didn't understand was, in my heart, they were now my responsibility, and I had to take care of them no matter the cost.

One day, Durad was playing football at Reggie McKenzie's field. As I sat on the porch, a neighbor's kid ran up to me and said, "Your brother got hurt!" I instantly took off running across the street and through the field. By the time I reached him, his eyes were already filled with tears, so I picked him up and carried him home, and I did my best to clean him up. That moment confirmed something I had already felt; I was their protector.

My siblings and I had to be enrolled in school, so Grandma began gathering all our school records, and when my birth certificate came back, I noticed that my name was spelled S-O-N-A. I didn't like the way it was spelled. It was odd because I didn't know anyone else with that name, and all I wanted was to fit in because I already felt different from everyone else.

Later on, Grandma took us to the clinic for a checkup. Dr. Saha looked at me and asked, "Do you know what your name means?" I shook my head. He said, "In my country, your name means gold or something precious." So, for the first time, I embraced my name because it no longer felt like something I needed to hide.

Our house was walking distance from Woodward Avenue, where there were plenty of stores: S.S. Kresge's, Woolworths, Sears, Highland Appliance, and many more. One day, while Subrina and I were walking down Woodward, two women approached us and asked, "Do you know who Jesus is?"

Subrina and I looked at each other, then back at them, and said, "No."

They then replied, "We have good news. Would you like to hear it?"

We nodded yes.

They began to tell us that Jesus is Lord, and He died on the cross for our sins, and on the third day He rose again. They also said that if we believed and asked God for forgiveness, we could become part of His family. We agreed, and they prayed over us that day.

In that moment, I felt something change inside of me. It felt like God had stepped into my life. But the strange thing is… we never saw those women again.

I have learned that even in those moments of silence, God is still speaking, and He will speak through whomever He chooses to.

192 Midland Street in Highland Park, Michigan.

Me, Subrina, Durad, Grandma, &
Auntie Eloise's daughter, Tisha

Chapter 5

THE FIGHT WITHIN

4 "For the weapons of our warfare are not carnal, but mighty through God to the pulling down of strong holds;)"

5 "Casting down imaginations, and every high thing that exalteth itself against the knowledge of God, and bringing into captivity every thought to the obedience of Christ;"
– 2 Corinthians 10:4-5 (KJV)

My grandmother worked as a CNA at Mount Carmel Hospital, and whenever she wasn't working, I was right by her side. I followed her so closely that she started calling me her shadow.

Uncle Larry worked in a factory and sold Amway products on the side. He always made sure there were plenty of pastries in the house, especially some donuts. Because of that, we nicknamed him Uncle Donut, and whenever he wasn't working, you could usually find him listening to sports on his portable radio.

Auntie Eloise worked at a doctor's office, and on the weekends, she cleaned the house while singing along to her favorite records. She loved artists like Natalie Cole, Lou Rawls, and Peaches & Herb. I always looked forward to hearing her hit those high notes that seemed to echo throughout the entire house.

Uncle Robert was finishing his last year of high school and worked part-time at Burger King. He was athletic, loved martial arts, and even trained some of the neighborhood's teenage boys. Not long after he graduated, he enlisted in the U.S. Navy. I remember feeling so proud when I told people that my uncle was in the Navy.

I spent a lot of time at Auntie Lillie's house; she was a blessing to be around. She was married, a homemaker, loved to read, and always sang her favorite song, *"Going to the Chapel of Love" by The Dixie Cups,* while cooking. I can still picture her curled up with a book, a cigarette in one hand and a Pepsi in the other.

Auntie Joyce was married and worked at the Detroit Osteopathic Hospital. I loved riding in the car with her while Chaka Khan's *"Tell Me Something Good"* played through the speakers. One thing I'll always remember about

Aunt Joyce is that she never missed celebrating someone's birthday.

Around 1980, Grandma and I were shopping at Sears when I saw Lester walking toward us. My heart started racing; my chest tightened so fast I could barely breathe. My Grandma grabbed my hand, but Lester didn't look at me. He only spoke to Grandma and asked about my sister, Lady. They exchanged phone numbers, and when he walked away, my Grandma looked at me and said, "Tina, breathe. It's going to be okay."

Seeing Lester at Sears was a traumatizing trigger that ripped open the wounds I hadn't yet healed from. It was so traumatic and overwhelming, and I didn't know how to cope or deal with that type of pain. So, my grandmother, doing what she believed was best at the time, admitted me to a children's mental hospital, where I stayed for about two months.

I didn't have the words for it then, but I know now I was carrying PTSD in my body long before I could understand what it was. I was carrying the weight of that trauma, and I didn't know how to release it. I had more questions than answers: How could Lester only serve three years? My Mama was gone, and why was he free? And to top it all off, he wanted to see my baby sister, Lady.

When the day came for Lady to go to his house, Lester knocked on the door. I was relieved that he didn't come inside. After they left, I asked Grandma, "How could she let the man who took my Mama come and get Lady?" She softly replied, "She was my daughter. We have to forgive and let God handle the rest." I told my grandmother that I could never forgive Lester. I would never see my mother again, and I was terrified that he might hurt Lady the same way he hurt me.

Anger, bitterness, and unforgiveness quickly grew inside of me. I kept reliving everything that happened on February 26th. Over and over, the trauma Lester caused replayed in my mind. I couldn't deal with the pain, so I started hanging around the wrong crowd, fighting, skipping school, and smoking cigarettes and marijuana. All the while, my grandmother was doing everything within her power to help me.

When summer arrived, my Grandma told me that my father's side of the family was having a family reunion, and if I wanted to go, and I said yes. My dad had always denied being my father, so at 14, I didn't even know who he was. His denial planted seeds of rejection, abandonment, and disappointment inside of me, so just the thought of meeting my father for the first time made me both nervous and excited.

My grandfather, his girlfriend, Miss Elaine, his mother, Grandma Effie, his daughter, Donna, and my half-sister, Roxy, all took the drive from Highland Park to St. Louis. When we arrived, Robert James was there, and if you have ever watched *Sanford and Son*, he reminded me of the character, Rollo.

Robert James to me was just a street guy who was known to be on and off drugs. He was a smooth talker and also involved in a few illegal things. When I first saw him, he introduced himself as my dad. I had never called any man 'dad' before, so when he spoke that word, it felt weird. Still, I met him and the rest of his family for the first time.

As years went on, I spiraled further out of control. I experimented with drugs like mescaline, crack, cocaine, heroin, and opioids. I began selling drugs and transporting them, and I searched for love in places it couldn't be found. I was promiscuous with the same and opposite sex, and I found myself aborting baby after baby.

The saying goes, "It takes a village to raise a child." Well, I had a village, and I was surrounded by people who loved me, but I couldn't see their love through my pain.

But through it all, I had one constant thing … a praying grandmother.

Me & Auntie Lillie

Uncle Robert

Uncle Larry

Me & Aunt Eloise

Me, Aunt Joyce & Uncle Larry

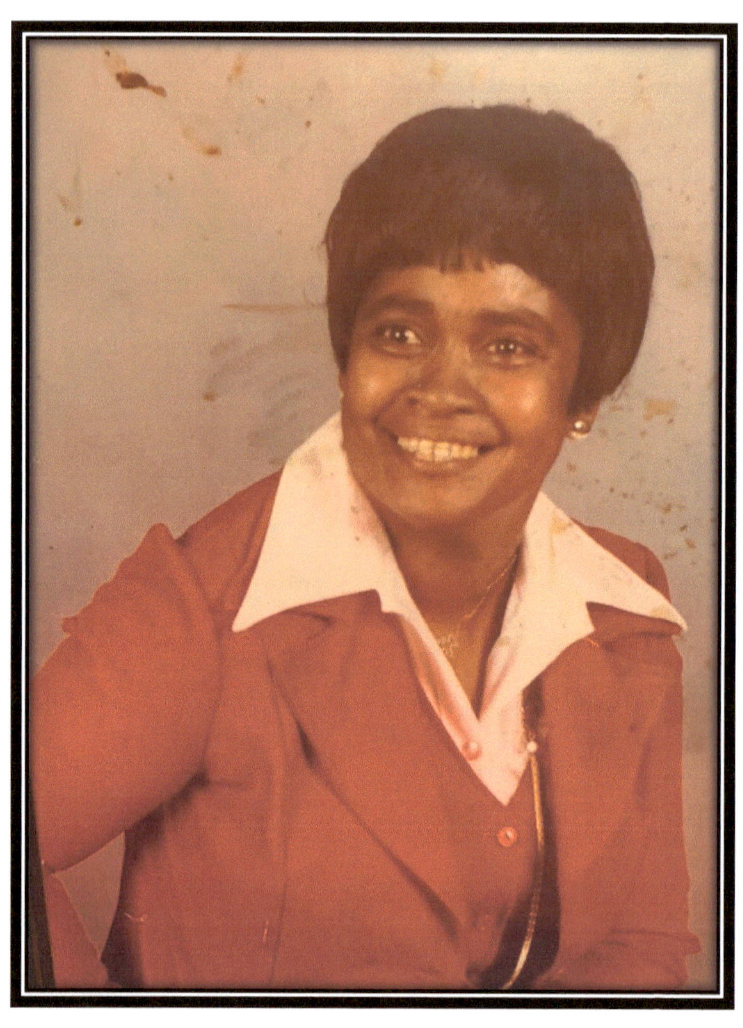

My Grandma

Roosevelt Noble (Grandfather)

Chapter 6

BLESSED AND FORGIVEN

1 "Blessed is the one
whose transgressions are forgiven,
whose sins are covered."

2 "Blessed is the one
whose sin the LORD *does not count against them*
and in whose spirit is no deceit." – Psalm 32:1-2 (NIV)

For many years, the life I lived was reckless, empty, and filled with a void. So, I take full responsibility for the pain I caused, physically, mentally, and emotionally, to myself and to others.

The shame of being molested kept me in bondage for many years. I didn't want to continuously think about the darkness, and the only way I felt I could escape the pain was to self-medicate. I became best friends with the drug, heroin, until one day in 1993, when I just got tired of being high. Thankfully, someone told me about a clinic that dispensed methadone to help me kick the addiction. So, I made up my mind to go.

On the first day, I was assessed by a doctor, and he said, "Do you see the people in the lobby?" I replied, "Yes." He went on to say, "You don't belong here, so I'm going to start you on 45 milligrams of methadone, and each week I'll reduce it by 2 milligrams so that you can kick this habit."

I also had to go to Narcotics Anonymous, and as everyone went around the room telling their drug of choice, I shared my drug of choice and everything that I had used. After I spoke, everyone looked at me with a smirk, as if to say, I don't believe you were ever on any drugs. Please don't get me wrong, by no means did I think I was better than anyone there. But when I look back, I can clearly see that God had plans for my life.

During the time of my recovery, I had many conversations with people who never exposed who had touched them. Still, I was appalled to hear the things they were told:

'You probably liked it.'

'Don't tell what happened in this house.' or

'I don't believe you.'

A lot of people in the black community don't believe in getting counseling; they just go through life as though it never happened.

As I was healing and being drawn closer to the Father God. I noticed that a lot of church leaders hadn't dealt with their trauma, and that really bothered me. One day, a coworker invited me to a faith-based intervention encounter workshop. The workshop was designed to confront and overcome traumatic experiences while helping you become strengthened, empowered, and encouraged as you walk in your life's journey.

One of the workshop's facilitators was Prophetess Veronica Carouthers. Oh, my goodness, this little lady was full of fire, and I was instantly drawn to her teaching. But what I didn't know was that God was leading me to my next assignment. A couple of days had passed, and I asked Prophetess Veronica Carouthers if she could mentor me, and she was honored to do so. And by 2024, I moved to Texas, where Prophetess resided. As of today, we have maintained a mentor-mentee relationship that has truly blessed me abundantly.

Looking back on my life, my turning point came when I finally decided to seek God with everything in me. Through prayer, reading His Word, and fasting, I began to learn His character and His heart for me. In that process, I chose to no longer allow my past to define my future. First, I had to forgive Lester, and that wasn't easy. I'm not sure what happened during his life, but I did hear that he passed away in 2008 of Dementia and Parkinson's Disease. But I surely hope he repented before he took his last breath.

My life has surely been a journey of joy and sorrow. My sister, Lady, was taken in 1993 in a massacre at her best friend's house. My brother Durad is happily married, Subrina is an Ordained Minister and an Entrepreneur, and Grandma quietly passed away in 2021. Unfortunately, life happens to us all; therefore, I pray that my story encourages someone to know that if I could make it through, so can you.

And just as gold must go through the fire to be purified, God allowed me to walk through the fire so that the old version of me could be burned away. And while I was in that refining process, God began shaping me for His purpose and preparing me to be used for His Kingdom. Today, I thank God for His mercy, His grace, and His divine forgiveness. My past may be part of my story, but it is no longer the author of my life.

"And the God of all grace, who called you to His eternal glory in Christ. After you have suffered a little while, He will Himself restore you and make you strong, firm, and steadfast. - 1 Peter: 5:10

Lady

My Grandma

Durad & his wife, Rose Marie

Me & my sister Subrina

Curtis Jackson (my grandfather/great uncle)

Me and my grandmother

Robert James (my dad)

Me & my granddad/great uncle

A Letter to My Mama

Dear Mama,

Even though you're gone on to be with the Lord, I feel compelled to write you this letter. For so long, I was angry that you had to leave us.

Mother's Day was hard.

A permission slip that needed to be signed by a parent was hard.

Your birthday was hard.

Each achievement without you was hard.

Knowing you weren't going to walk through the door was hard.

I miss you, and the one important lesson that you taught me was to protect the family. Mama, I understand that you did your best as a mother. You carried me for 9 months, and I will always love, honor, and cherish you.

Continue to rest till we meet again.

www.ingramcontent.com/pod-product-compliance
Lightning Source LLC
LaVergne TN
LVHW052258100826
845147LV00001B/76

* 9 7 8 1 9 5 2 7 5 2 4 3 8 *